2014
PEOPLE'S
CLIMATE MARCH

PROTEST!
March for **CHANGE**

by Joyce Markovics

CHERRY LAKE PRESS

Published in the United States of America by Cherry Lake Publishing Group
Ann Arbor, Michigan
www.cherrylakepublishing.com

Reading Adviser: Marla Conn, MS Ed., Literacy specialist, Read-Ability, Inc.
Content Adviser: Emilye Crosby, PhD
Book Designer: Ed Morgan

Photo Credits: Wikimedia Commons, cover and title page; © a katz/Shutterstock, 4–5; © a katz/Shutterstock, 6; © Osugi/Shutterstock, 7; © Johan Swanepoel/Shutterstock, 8–9; © Designua/Shutterstock, 9; © EAKARAT BUANOI/Shutterstock, 10; © capaulfell/Shutterstock, 11 top; © Alohaflaminggo/Shutterstock, 11 bottom; © Dipak Shelare/Shutterstock, 12; © freepik.com, 13; Wikimedia Commons, 14; © Alexandros Michailidis/Shutterstock, 15; Wikimedia Commons, 16; © a katz/Shutterstock, 17; © Erica Violet Lee, 18 left; Wikimedia Commons, 18 right; © andyparker72/Shutterstock, 19; © a katz/Shutterstock, 19; © Daniele COSSU/Shutterstock, 21.

Cherry Lake Press is an imprint of Cherry Lake Publishing Group.

Library of Congress Cataloging-in-Publication Data

Names: Markovics, Joyce L., author.
Title: 2014 people's climate march / by Joyce Markovics.
Description: Ann Arbor, Michigan : Cherry Lake Publishing, 2021. | Series:
   Protest! march for change | Includes bibliographical references and
   index. | Audience: Grades 2-3
Identifiers: LCCN 2020038470 (print) | LCCN 2020038471 (ebook) | ISBN
   9781534186323 (hardcover) | ISBN 9781534186408 (paperback) | ISBN
   9781534186484 (pdf) | ISBN 9781534186569 (ebook)
Subjects: LCSH: Environmentalism—Juvenile literature. | Climatic
   changes—Juvenile literature. | Environmental protection—Juvenile
   literature.
Classification: LCC GE195.5 .M365 2021 (print) | LCC GE195.5 (ebook) |
   DDC 363.738/74—dc23
LC record available at https://lccn.loc.gov/2020038470
LC ebook record available at https://lccn.loc.gov/2020038471

Printed in the United States of America
Corporate Graphics

C**O**NTENTS

FOR THE PLANET

Thousands of people squeezed together on the streets of New York City. Excitement filled the air. As they marched, they beat on drums. A rainbow of banners flew above their heads. Some of the signs read "You Control Climate Change" and "Save Our Earth!"

It was September 21, 2014, the day of the People's Climate March. Around 300,000 people marched together that day. It was the biggest **protest** against climate change in U.S. history!

People young and old of every color stood side by side. Parents marched with their children. "We're here as a family for the future of our kids," said one family. The protesters chanted, "What do we want? **Justice!** When do we want it? Now!"

A group called the People's Climate Movement had planned the march. But it was regular people who made it happen. They joined forces to raise awareness about the dangers of climate change. They also marched to pressure government leaders to take action.

The United Nations is made up of different countries. The organization works to keep peace and solve problems in the world.

The march took place 2 days before a big **international** meeting about climate. It was called the United Nations Climate Summit.

CLIMATE CRISIS

What exactly is climate change? People burn fossil fuels, such as oil and coal, to get energy. The energy powers our cars and makes electricity for our homes. When fossil fuels are burned, a gas called carbon dioxide is released into the air.

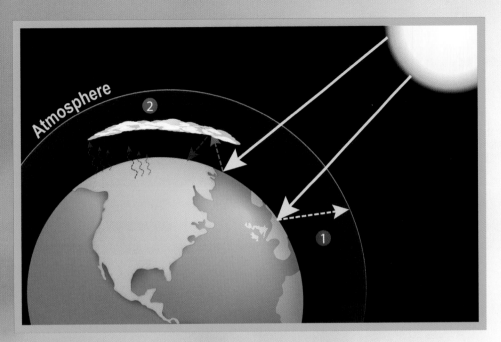

This diagram shows the greenhouse effect.

Carbon dioxide traps heat in the **atmosphere**, much like a greenhouse traps heat. This is known as the greenhouse effect. As a result, Earth's climate is changing, and the air and oceans are getting warmer.

The climate has changed a lot during Earth's history. These changes occurred naturally. But now, people's actions are causing the climate to change and are harming the planet in the process.

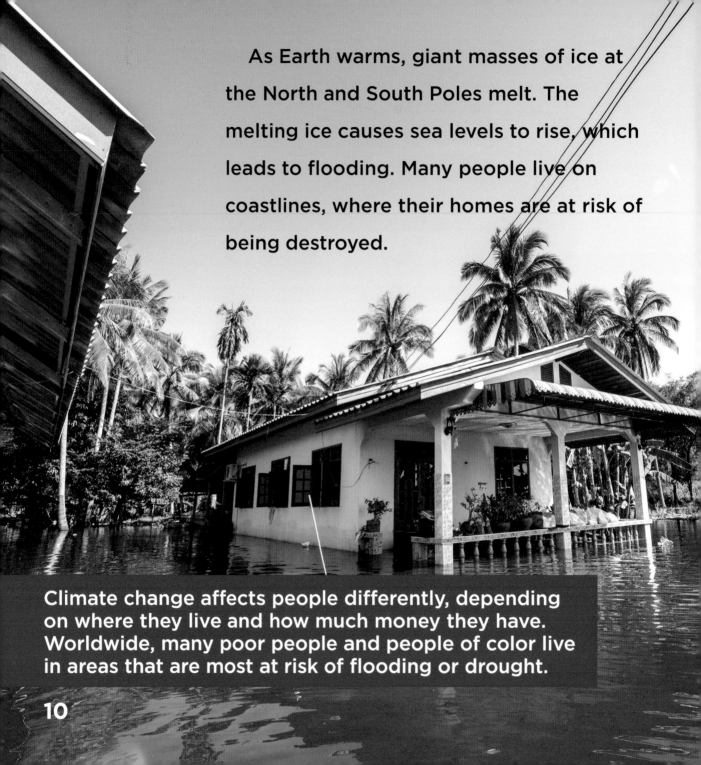

As Earth warms, giant masses of ice at the North and South Poles melt. The melting ice causes sea levels to rise, which leads to flooding. Many people live on coastlines, where their homes are at risk of being destroyed.

Climate change affects people differently, depending on where they live and how much money they have. Worldwide, many poor people and people of color live in areas that are most at risk of flooding or drought.

As the planet gets warmer, thousands of animals, such as snow leopards, are at risk of dying out. Many animals have already gone extinct.

Warmer oceans pass heat high into the atmosphere. This can bring about more powerful storms. It can also cause less rain to fall in certain areas. This can dry up the land, causing drought, and lead to food shortages.

Since 2015, India and other countries have been affected by severe drought. Farmers are struggling to keep their crops alive and families fed.

11

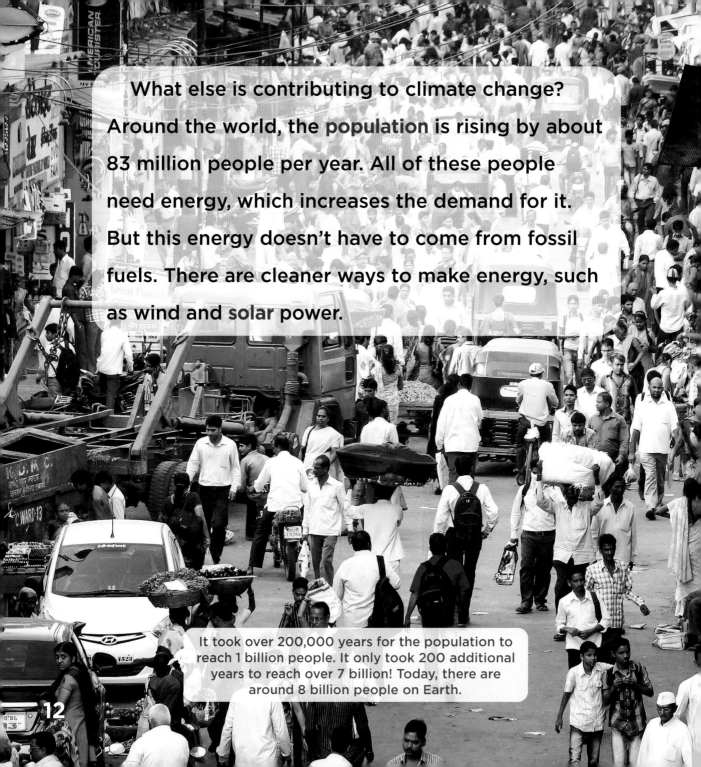

What else is contributing to climate change? Around the world, the population is rising by about 83 million people per year. All of these people need energy, which increases the demand for it. But this energy doesn't have to come from fossil fuels. There are cleaner ways to make energy, such as wind and solar power.

It took over 200,000 years for the population to reach 1 billion people. It only took 200 additional years to reach over 7 billion! Today, there are around 8 billion people on Earth.

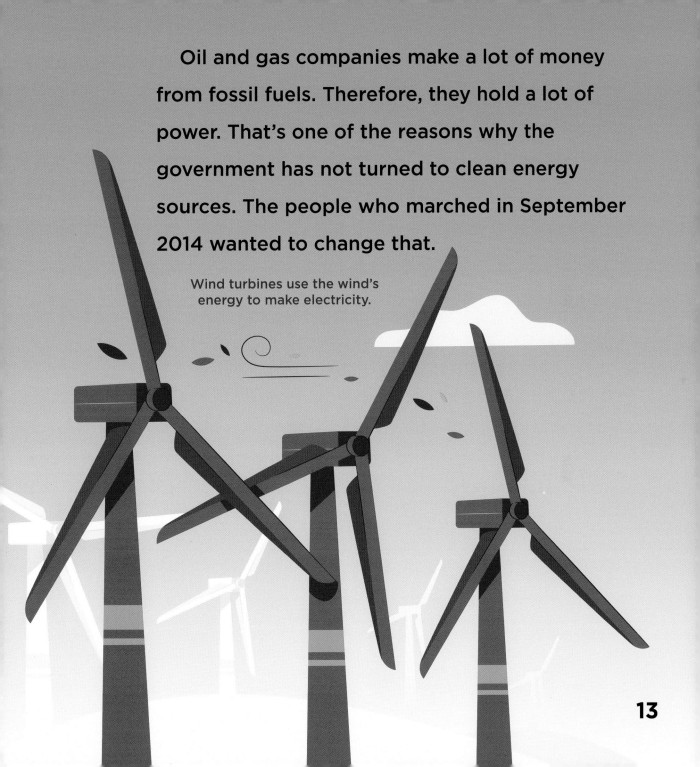

Oil and gas companies make a lot of money from fossil fuels. Therefore, they hold a lot of power. That's one of the reasons why the government has not turned to clean energy sources. The people who marched in September 2014 wanted to change that.

Wind turbines use the wind's energy to make electricity.

THE MARCH

Writer and activist Bill McKibben was one of the organizers of the march. In May 2014, he wrote an article calling climate change "the biggest crisis our civilization has ever faced." He talked about individuals taking action.

Bill McKibben

McKibben spoke of the need for "a loud movement—one that gives our 'leaders' permission to actually lead, and then scares them into doing so." Many heard McKibben's powerful message and wanted to get involved. They showed up by the thousands in New York to march.

The starting point of the People's Climate March was Central Park. Six distinct groups made up the march. At the front were people most affected by climate change, including indigenous people. Families and environmental organizations followed them. Then different protest groups, scientists, and interfaith organizations came last.

At 11:30 a.m., waves of people moved downtown. Some of the marchers were famous actors. They used their fame to shine a spotlight on climate change. Others were well-known activists. Many spoke passionately at the march.

Although the People's Climate March was based in New York City, another 300,000 people marched around the world.

Erica Violet Lee, a **First Nations** woman, spoke on behalf of indigenous people. She's part of a movement called Idle No More. Started in 2012, the women-led group pushes for laws that protect the environment. It **advocates** for indigenous people who have been **oppressed** and pushed aside by governments.

Erica Violet Lee

Lee said that any violence against Earth is violence against indigenous people. "I'm here for those who struggle every day back home," she said. "This is for the women who are afraid to speak but who do anyway. You and me, we're the revolution."

A First Nations marcher

NEXT STEPS

The 2014 march inspired people and led to other big protests. In all, nearly 1 million people have taken to the streets to fight climate change. Bill McKibben said that individuals must "join a movement big enough to change the politics."

Americans can vote for leaders who support clean energy.

Greta Thunberg is a vegan, which means she doesn't eat or use animal products. A vegan diet is better for the environment because plants require less energy and resources to grow.

Greta Thunberg was only 11 years old when the march was held. But four years later, the Swedish teenager became an internationally known climate activist. One thing she's done is plan "climate strikes" where millions of students leave school to draw attention to climate change. "We deserve a safe future. . . . Is that really too much to ask?" Thunberg said.

Greta Thunberg has also met with dozens of world leaders to urge them to address climate change.

TIMELINE

2003
January 3
Greta Thunberg is born.

2012
December
The group Idle No More is formed by four women, including three First Nations women.

2014
May
Bill McKibben writes an article in *Rolling Stone* magazine about climate change and invites readers to the September march.

September 21
The People's Climate March takes place in New York City.

2018
August
Greta Thunberg organizes her first climate strike.

December
Greta Thunberg makes a now famous speech about climate change at the United Nations climate change conference called COP 24.

GLOSSARY

activist (AK-tuh-vist) a person who fights for a cause

advocates (AD-vuh-kayts) supports or speaks in favor of something

atmosphere (AT-muhs-feer) the mixture of gases surrounding Earth

civilization (siv-uh-lih-ZAY-shuhn) society

climate change (KLYE-mit CHAYNJ) the warming of Earth's air and oceans due to changes in weather and weather patterns, happening because of human activity

First Nations (FURST NAY-shuhnz) American Indian people from Canada

fossil fuels (FAH-suhl FYOO-uhlz) coal, oil, or natural gas, formed from the remains of plants and animals that died millions of years ago

indigenous (in-DIJ-uh-nuhs) describing people who are the earliest known to live in a particular place

interfaith (IN-tur-fayth) involving people of different religions

international (in-tur-NASH-uh-nuhl) involving countries around the world

justice (JUHS-tis) the quality of being fair and good

oppressed (uh-PRESD) subjected to harsh and unfair treatment

population (pop-yuh-LAY-shuhn) the total number of people living in a place

protest (PROH-test) an organized public gathering to influence or change something

revolution (rev-uh-LOO-shuhn) an overthrow of the government or a system by the people governed

shortages (SHOR-tij-iz) situations where there is not enough of something that is needed or expected

solar (SOH-lur) having to do with the sun

FIND OUT MORE

Books

Henderson, Leah. *Together We March: 25 Protest Movements That Marched into History.* New York: Atheneum Books, 2021.

Hudson, Wade, and Cheryl Willis Hudson, eds. *We Rise, We Resist, We Raise Our Voices*. New York: Crown Books for Young Readers, 2018.

Kluger, Jeffrey. *Raise Your Voice: 12 Protests That Shaped America*. New York: Philomel Books, 2020.

Websites

American Museum of Natural History—What Is Climate Change?
   https://www.amnh.org/explore/ology/climate-change

Peoples Climate Movement
   https://peoplesclimate.org

Zinn Education Project—Stories from the Climate Crisis: A Mixer
   https://www.zinnedproject.org/materials/climate-crisis-mixer

INDEX

ABOUT THE AUTHOR

Joyce Markovics is a writer and history buff. She loves learning about people and telling their stories. This book is dedicated to her mother, Carol, a powerful advocate for the environment, and to all the people who march for a more just future.